IN TIME

In Time

Michael Anania

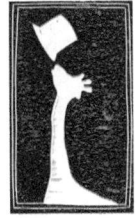

MadHat Press
Cheshire, Massachusetts

MadHat Press
MadHat Incorporated
PO Box 422, Cheshire, MA 01225

Copyright © 2024 Michael Anania
All rights reserved

The Library of Congress has assigned
this edition a Control Number of
2024933471

ISBN 978-1-952335-78-5 (paperback)

Words by Michael Anania
Cover image by Lee Avison and Marc Vincenz
Cover design by Marc Vincenz

www.MadHat-Press.com

First Printing
Printed in the United States of America

Other Books by Michael Anania:

New Poetry Anthology
The Color of Dust
Set/Sorts
Riversongs
The Red Menace (fiction)
Constructions/Variations
Two Poems
The Sky at Ashland
Gardening the Skies
In Plain Sight: Obsessions, Morals
    and Domestic Laughter (essays)
Selected Poems
In Natural Light
Once Again, Flowered
Sounds/Snow
Per Enzo Agostino
Turnings
Heat Lines
Continuous Showings
Nightsongs and Clamors
This and That

For Dianne, all these many musics

Table of Contents

I.

Instead Of	3
Northern Lights (Minneapolis 2020)	5
Song for a Dire Time	6
All This While	7
"Strange Forms with Fancy"	9
San Antonio Piece	11
A Dirge, of Sorts	12
"Your Fancy and Your Sight"	13
Easter 2022	15
Uvalde	16

II.

Gli Ucelli (The Birds)	19
Six Variations on a Theme by William Schumann	25
Something Like Sorrow	31
Covering Stan Getz	32
Predicaments	33
After a Photograph	34
What Percy Said	35
Here Comes the Night	36
Harvest Time	37
At the Lincoln Gardens in Chicago with Roy Fisher	38
Parallel Lines	39

III.

Memory Songs	43
Walking Home, Summer 1960	49
In Light of	50
New Year's Day 2013	51
Song	53

To and Fro	54
A Shard	56
Late Itinerary	57
Plains Song	58
As It Were	59
At Argos	60
Cañada Vista	61
This Broken Song	62
Riverrun	64
"*Oppi, ne metuas ...*"	67

IV.

Hours and Days	71
"The people know the present"	77
Reprieve	79
First Snow	80
Heading Out	81
At Purchase	82
Idle Thoughts in Troubled Circumstances	84
In Myriads	87
A Redbud in Central Ohio	89
Another Iowa Homage	90
Omaha Appendices VII	92
Omaha Appendices VIII	94

V.

Prologue and Songs from a Libretto

Prologue	97
Sad Eyes and Smiles	98
Polly's First Song	99
Mac's Confession	101
Polly's Song	103
Duet	104
Jenny's Song	106

Dancer's Song	108
Notes	111
Acknowledgments	113
About the Author	115

The way we imagine is often more instructive than what we imagine.
—Bachelard

Run on, you spindles, turning the thread.
—Catullus

I

Instead Of

> *we are defined by the absences that enclose us*
> —George Hitchcock

leaned forward into what?
  the six feet now demanded
    of us; unsheltered in place,

America seems empty
  once again—streets, sidewalks,
    the schoolyard I pass each day;

no one is hurrying through
  this afternoon's downpour,
    paper bags of leaves soak at the curb;

homeless, uncared for, aging,
  we get by on alcohol and bitter
    root, this spring's first flowering;

petals spill from Flora's
  lips like the wishes that close
    the evening news, Primavera

in her own lock-down,
  the Arno, Times Square,
    the Grand Canal, each plaza

everywhere; this is not
  the one world we had hoped
    for, what was photographed

Michael Anania

from the Sea of Tranquility
   and seen whole for the first time,
      the oceans' blue and cloud white,

the dark shapes we live on,
   have names for and call our
      own and that vast, blank space,

the absence of air and its
   accompanying light, of sound
      and substance, of all that gives

us place; *é stato un piacere*
   sentire la tua voce, Maurizio,
      reaching with your son toward us;

victory is in the voice itself,
   the arc of song we ride briefly
      with you across this ingathering night

Northern Lights

(Minneapolis 2020)

fire is the weapon of the unarmed,
anger's essential element;
it dances into the night, their hands
uplifted to it, arms in silhouette;
resembling the forms of dreams,
they move, ancient and ecstatic
against the daily fear, against
silence or muttered capitulations

Michael Anania

Song for a Dire Time

how can we, even
   in quiet moments,
      suppose that things

arrange themselves
   for us, a compliant
      world, its flowerings

meant to be seen
   as consolations,
      if not dispelling

fear, then somehow
   superseding it, wishes,
      mere hankerings grown

and brightly reaching
   toward us this April in
      all other things undone

All This While

in lilac shadows
   —Giuseppe Ungaretti (1916)

where among these losses—
hunched figures single file,
grey dawn or soiled evening—
do you find them, "water
droplets like gemstones,"
moments perfected from dread?

I return, as always,
to light and shadow, strains
of familiar music, lyrics
filled with love and absence;
we are between wars, kneel
into our own despairs;

the wasp hovering here means
only to find a brief rest,
a lizard in silhouette nods
once, then moves away,
branches shagged with ball moss
catch the afternoon sun;

intensity is, as always ,
the space between singular
and plural, the lists—not
lists even, mere numbers
of the dead, the night bug tick
of infusion, the huff of intubation;

Michael Anania

we wait, imagining each
breath might bring our own virus;
numbers, once again, how many
breaths remain before your
number's up, "take that, buster,"
a final darkness without a dawn;

stare, then, at what is close,
what shines in the moment, its
movements slight and accidental;
"I wish I may," heart sick,
"I wish I might," nod once,
hover through sun and shade;

the lilac blooms in memory.
not in the dooryard, but
at the kitchen door, spring,
all those other springs, and loss
the sum that age contends with,
particulate and strange

"Strange Forms with Fancy"

trial and error—how is
it we manage these days,
all touch withheld from us?

the cactus on my walk is
opening its waxen buds,
my mock orange is in full

bloom; at some distance
peonies have pushed up
through winter's crust

glory-of-the-snow is
snowed in once again,
wind flowers and scilla;

distances marked by
this season's urgencies,
a handful of spring air,

my dear, these changes
we think of as time are
directionless, purpose,

an invention we have
agreed to, the area
seen under the green

Michael Anania

curve of leaf and stem,
cloud and cloud shadow
moving in their own ways;

a fistful of microbes,
a deep breath counted
out now; all that seems

to be starting up again,
the long evening's bright
reach ends, its ending

a meteor shower, seen
only as it extinguishes
itself, ourselves, embers

as well, quietly separate
beneath the distant slow
burning fires of the stars

San Antonio Piece

under the trellis, she said,
in the arbor, behind the viburnum,
between the yews, beside the elm,
next to the oak, along the hedge

Why "she said," and not merely
because it was a "she," even then
you have a choice, so "she"?
perhaps, "one said," not "he,"
which would be a betrayal
of sorts, not "they" either,
though these days there is
a social preference that elects
the plural as somehow neutral.
Why does anyone have to say it?
Because "she" or "he" or "one,"
even, give it a presence it
would not otherwise have;
in some way "she," over-
gendered as it is, is more
certain, which perhaps betrays
my own disposition, that "she"
is more likely to propose
an ontology than "one" or "he,"
and so make that deliberate
play of prepositions seem
less completely arbitrary.
Just now, a sparrow flies up to
the fence rail. Unattributed, thus,
as a statement, implicitly mine.

Michael Anania

A Dirge, of Sorts

in early autumn
the brick makers are
playing doo wop on
a lime streaked boom box;
the foreman wearing
an Edelbrock tee shirt,
proposing tuned headers
and reckless speed,
America at work
as we sit nearby
listening to the numbers
of this day's
dead and dying

"Your Fancy and Your Sight"

for Diana Matthias

"only nothing increases," as though
an area of darkness grew daily
and we stood at its edges, reasoning
something like fate, our impending
losses, death, disease, all that our fears
propose to us, "cursëd end and heavy
chance"; wish no more, they have
counted fifty Empire State asteroids
hurdling toward us, sure obliteration
blazing through the night sky

and yet you walk through my dreams
dressed in pastels, your hair somewhat
carelessly pulled back, a Chinese
painting in black and white behind you;
grace arrives as needed, violet and sage,
your death, ours not that far behind;
is it more than mere duration, time's
apparent simplicity, beginning to end,
the first cry, fervent and demanding,
the last, a catch in the throat or a sigh

still, all that you see, have seen, has
its own rich moment, moments woven,
things the eye's dreaming shuttle weaves
together in sleep, gardens, rivers, streams;
where does it go, all that subtlety,
the fancy that's made of sight or fancy
giving its own intricate shapes to sight;

Michael Anania

who will play Actaeon, who Diana
did disguise, wander in tree shade
to his own ending and its ironies?

there is a figure that reoccurs
in Corot, a young woman reading;
once, leaning against a tree, she is
not so much a part of the scene as
its maker, all that the book and her
reading propose—a classical nude,
her hair tended by a fully clothed
servant, Diana, once again—these
are the measures destined for us,
things imagined and reimagined

bright chance or chances, unrelenting,
archaic songs, their creatures manifest,
dear heart, tracing with us the known
world's possibilities; how and why
is it sweet, the owl of Suffolk,
or Hesperus smooth, qualities
acquiring substance, rather than
the other way around; we make
our way, make way, through memory's
passages, line by line, color by color

Easter 2022

along this Texas highway, parked cars
families taking pictures of children
sitting or lying down in bluebonnets,
girls in white dresses, boys in their
Communion suits, bright faces, lifted
on a wave of white-centered flowers

near Lviv, cars are left at the roadside,
mothers and their children trudge toward
Poland, eyes fixed ahead, behind them
mortars open their steel and cordite petals;
tattered recessional, this April the stone
at the church door, smoke-stained, unturned,

motankas, linen angels, singed and burnt;
there are no guardians in this world, no pause
for them, no rest along the way; this is death's
resurrection, fields of rubble, sown with
cartridge casings and unexploded rounds,
bodies robed, hooded in black plastic;

we greet the Spring and all its figures
of hope—bluebonnets, Indian paintbrush,
fiddlehead ferns uncurling into the light—
then, daily, news photographs, footage of
charred buildings, garden plots of broken glass,
a girl's body bent across a bloodstained curb

Michael Anania

Uvalde

There is nothing any of us can say,
Nothing of use in the political drone,
For parents waiting for the DNA

Of bodies shredded, faces gone; pray
For our own forgiveness, stammer, moan.
There is nothing any of us can say

To stations of white crosses, their array
Of photographs, bright faces known
Only from cotton swabs of DNA.

Listen, listen for the sounds of play,
For skip rope rhymes; we're left alone
With nothing of any use to say.

Is this our innocence's final day,
Our new Eden all weeds now and overgrown?
Should we count the stripes in our own DNA

To find what part we play in death, lay
Flowers by the schoolyard, kneel, lie prone?
There is nothing any of us can say
That's not said, mutely, by their DNA.

II

Gli Ucelli (The Birds)

for Margherita Harwell

*many birds fly here and there
in sunlight and not all are omens*

I.

this morning's birds,
    Tuscan, pecking at the season's
        last surviving persimmons,

diosperi, here, god's fire, winter
    orange, like flames, votive, along
        bare branches, *buon Natale*, still;

which birds are these, then,
    blackbirds, swallows or swifts,
        kaladóon, hirundo, speaking

into the chill morning, their
    struggle against the fruit,
        raucous, wings flailing;

sleep is a kind of flight,
    a lift into the thinner air,
        the forward press of dreams;

Vinci, just one hillside
    west, the Codex and its
        birds, inked marginalia,

Michael Anania

    how the tail is lifted
        as the head descends,
            the quickness of the thrust

    downward or the wings'
        recovery, differing among
            different species, their rush,

    prisms and levers, how
        the wingtip is drawn in
            to lessen the body's strain,

    vectors and hinged parts,
        wind drawn out in lines
            that trail in ink behind them

II.

Fermi and Respighi at sea
   together, a passage from Rio
      to Genoa, wavetips, the South

Atlantic sun, day after day
   in deck chairs; side by side
      they talked Italian politics,

laughed at Il Duce's plan
   to give cash bonuses to parents
      who would name their babies after him,

the poor south—Calabria, Puglia
   Sicily—filled with little Benitos
      and Benitas, a kind of immortality;

eventually Fermi posed
   his question, what he had been saving,
      Can you explain music in terms of physics?

Respighi said he would think
   about it; if I had the training, he said,
      the vocabulary, I could, I suppose, describe

the vibration of sounds in air, how
   it moves outward in all directions,
      how it is altered, however slightly,

Michael Anania

    by the surfaces it collides with,
        hard, soft, flat, curved, various,
            how these vibrations enter the ear

and in turn vibrate the ear drum,
    but all that would describe any sound,
        mere noise, speech, the engines beneath us;

in the Conservatorio in Rome,
    he said the next day, is a Roman
        statue of a boy, leaning toward

two chickens carved onto the same
    pedestal, his right hand extended
        has two or three seeds carved onto it

and there are a few seeds carved
    onto the stone pedestal in front
        of the chickens, his hair sways

forward across his cheeks,
    his short toga raised above
        the backs of his bare thighs;

the physics of this sculpture
    is uncomplicated, the boy,
        his toga, the seeds in his hand,

the seeds on the pedestal,
   the chickens and the seeds
      carved in front of them

are all cut from the same stone,
   so the molecules and the atoms
      are all the same, the hardness

of the stone and its stability
   can be described and quantified,
      its weight, its mass, its volume,

but none of that would speak
   to the moment the sculptor spared
      for us, the implicit fall of the seeds

from the boy's hand to the ground,
   his forward motion and the feeding
      chicken's urgent peck and scratch;

the action is ours, not the stone's,
   as is its stillness, and whatever
      spins inside it, whatever clutches

molecule to molecule, may be
   essential but is irrelevant to
      that chiseled ancient moment;

Michael Anania

I have written imitations
   of birdsongs for strings,
      oboes and flutes, for entire

orchestras, have written
   the struggle and glide
      of birds in flight, Enrico;

the players play, note
   after note, each vanishing into
      the next; sound is my stone;

time is the shape it takes
   in air, like flight, always
      memory and anticipation,

neither quite hand or seed
   but the space between one
      and the other, quick as thought

Six Variations on a Theme by Robert Schumann

I.

as though in quiet moments we
believed in the divinity of dreams,
each thing in our field of vision
grown random, then purposeful,
giving our wayward fancies shape

II.

basked all afternoon in the tropic sun,
evening sharply chilled on your skin,
grace in the moment marked by phosphors
gleaned from the water's brightening
approach, this wave and the next

III.

epyllion, set forth at least, an image drawn
gives way in time to swell after swell,
glows in streaks along sea honed lap-strakes,
all bent now to their oars as the sail
billows, the sheets drawn tight and sweating

IV.

gradual, her pardon, one self, the other
gone into Egypt, that war, not hers, made
as they so often are out of phantoms,
belief is beauty's darkest legacy, blood,
even now, helpless in these complexities

V.

grace in the moment, unsuffering us,
all these wishes, a broad sea, landfall
beckoning, city once again shining,
each of the deadly fires put out, the child we
grieve for bent across the curbside no more

VI.

a chance to turn away, perhaps, to take
back all that is still being lost to us, seaway
etched in foam, paths now scuffed toward refuge,
go down into the underworld, where all these
glyphs left behind in rubble are understood

Something Like Sorrow

for Dianne

what is it age requires of us
beyond simple endurance
and memory's implicit sorrows,
forgiveness perhaps, simple
pleasures and complex sentiments?
this evening's saxophonist, so
impatient, as though no
space could be left unfilled,
not a single note unfollowed;
we could have told him
that music, like age, is space
and silence; something like sorrow
waits in the air, something
riffs tinged with melody
could redeem, all the past's
reproaches set aside

Michael Anania

Covering Stan Getz

a line in time, time
curved, held and bent;

we struggle with
the moment as though

it were a shell we
could pry open

with our finger-
nails, releasing

something bright,
soft and pliant,

the air quick
and filled with it

Predicaments

gulls this evening
against the roseate
western sky; wishes
like songs, unsettle me

as though the future
were an oddly plausible
lyric, hidden like melody
in jazz, something you

eventually recognize;
part of its delight is
lifting the familiar
out of the strange

Michael Anania

After an Old Photograph

New Year's Eve with
Ella at the Savoy,
1940 vibrating through
the still air these
eighty years, the joy
she takes in her own
song, how she turns
her lips slightly,
a brief smile bending
the note to her will,
"starlit night," imagining
all that love imagines there

What Percy Said

for Jeffrey Allen

it isn't a question
of thought or action

but thought in action,
the reach of it, this

incessant present,
up is down, down up,

the moment's reach
just there and in time

Michael Anania

Here Comes the Night

"wait," she said,
the sea rising and falling,
shadows lengthening
   "what sea?"
if day is a series of
instruments, would evening
be a cello or in the woodwinds,
a bassoon, in the brass, who
knows, a baritone horn?
   "what sea?"
it doesn't matter, it's
a sea with waves rising,
foam-edged, and falling,
the nearby shadows getting
longer, the Tyrrhenian maybe
   "and she?"
she is in the poem, a voice,
trying, as we all do,
to hold back the dark, if
only for a moment or two

Harvest Time

after Pharoah Sanders

not yet antiphonal,
this early autumn, things
waiting, like strings the air
anticipates, chill
morning, calloused hands

and bent shoulders; what
is this long dreamy sentence,
sympathy or praise? we can
propose—and do—flight,
meditation, labor above

broken soil or weighted
branches; quick now, each day
retreating, baskets turned
out onto truck beds, all
those familiar inequities,

thorns and brambles, furrow
after furrow, tree line
and cornstalk, evening dew
caught in spider silk and along
larva threads; the Angelus?

probably not, but joy
nonetheless, this ingathering;
it is not a question of form
but presence, the fields fallow
now, and song gleaned from them

Michael Anania

At the Lincoln Gardens in Chicago with Roy Fisher

or rather in its empty space,
time, the city's relentless undoing,
here, then, the Twenties recalled—
King Oliver's Creole Jazz Band,
Armstrong, Jimmy Noone, Bill Johnson—
there just past the broken sidewalk
spikeweeds like table lamps
and leaning in Gene Krupa,
Benny Goodman, Bud Freeman,
Jimmy McPartland and Joe Sullivan;
this was the prospect in sound
they came to, 31st Street, white teenaged
sons of European immigrants;
co-option, my friend Pope, called it,
Sullivan tracing Lil Hardin's fingerings
against his thigh, Goodman breathing
with Noone, McPartland with Armstrong,
what they gathered in and carried away,
footfall and stride, New Orleans angled,
inflected by Chicago, taken up, then
passed around, phrased, rephrased,
New York, Paris, London, Birmingham,
each hand, each breath making its own
way out of what was first heard here;
in music, once known, like arc light
searing the retina, is known forever

Parallel Lines

"Michael," the pianist shouted,
"get in here and fuck me." It was,
after all, a dream and I was
thirty years younger and so I did,
though in her Eastern European
accent, it sounded like "get in here
and folk me," which might have required
costumes and dancing, wooden shoes even
and a measure of ethnic sensitivity.
And "she" became "you" and "yours,"
and "I" became "me" and "mine,"
which can happen in both fucking
and folking, alike, a grammar
of self and need. I had been thinking
about the Diabelli Variations, listened
to Pollini and Brendel, each satisfying
in its own way, Brendel precise, crisp,
Pollini with a kind of *bel canto* sway,
but this pianist, given her accent,
was likely Maria Yudina, Russian,
in photographs always darkly brooding,
always rebellious, she would interrupt
her own concerts to read banned poems
by exiled poets, Pasternak among them.
In 1944 she played Mozart's
Piano Concerto 23 on Moscow radio.
Stalin was moved by the performance
and asked for a recording, but it was
a live performance, not recorded.
Because Baria never disappointed

the boss, that night the NKVD assembled
an orchestra in a recording studio,
brought in Maria Yudina
and a conductor who was so nervous
about making a mistake while
playing for Stalin that he collapsed
and had to be replaced. Maria played
through the night, measure after measure.
Stalin sent her 20,000 rubles. She wrote
thanking him for the money, adding
that he was a disgrace to Russia
and had injured the Russian people;
she would pray, she said, that the Lord
might forgive him these and other sins
and that she had given the money
to the church where she worshiped.
The great surprise here is that
Stalin took no action against her.
and was listening to the recording
the night he died, which presumably
is why in a comic movie she
is credited with killing Stalin.
There is a recording of Maria
playing the Diabelli Variations,
not as crisp as Brendel or as moving
as Pollini, though it may be
the fault of the recording, but how
that explains the crude eroticism
of the dream is beyond me.

III

Memory Songs

after Meredith Monk

I.

"mandragora incense
   and a witch's cradle,"
Giovanni, Johannes
   the known world
circumscribed, Demagora,
   demons and angels;

the Atlantic before me
   that September morning
so long ago, rising,
   a nurse shark beached,
its back and fins intact,
   its insides alive with crabs

not archaic demons,
   Giovanni, but the effects
of international trade conflict
   on production and costs,
water resources, bananas,
   coffee and simple grains

lekythos, sacramental oil
   for the dead, three of them,
Leon, Helike and Demagora
   depicted on the jar's clay lid,
the moment of passage, though
   it is unclear who has died

Michael Anania

    I thought that day I had
        invented her, a name only,
    out of Blake or Graves, a myth,
        equal to loss or yearning,
    the almost unimaginable
        reach of the sea, the shark

    crabs feeding there, surplus
        value is death's offering,
    decay plus toil, enormous
        the land's tragedy; they bend
    to both the seed and its fruit
        scoring the field with song

II.

which Zoas will I wake to,
   the sand's breath all around,
"turning his eyes outward
   to self," the sea, then, laboring
at the shore, the stark ambiguity
   of wave form, shark and crab

what is the lesson after all?
   abundance or need
or the inevitability of loss,
   yearning's intolerable reach,
sand, the sea's wear, these
   dunes, its long consequence

Demagora, Leon's hand
   clutching hers, Helike looking on;
the oil, we guess, was there
   to ease her passage or his,
cultivation and the patience
   of harvest, press and strain

in Taverna in Calabria
   Johannes drew out the known
world in hemispheres, dark
   land-falls, oceans in blue tempera,
gave names and features
   to the night's lithe demons

Michael Anania

Giovanni in Damascus
   measuring water against
produce, in Honduras
   the tantalus of distant
markets against the way
   fruits ripen in the sun

loss and gain, Demagora;
   I scribbled your name, there
at the sea's edge to no
   great purpose and added
Johannes' *De Naturum Daemonum*,
   and the figure of the dead shark

III.

whatever is spared time's
   persistent wear, scraps
and tatters, names imagined
   or real or real and then imagined,
a scene bobbing to the surface,
   vivid, unexpected, clear

like music, each note, each
   chord, its own expectation
confirming itself, the present
   leaning forward with a backward
glance, that distant shore, wind,
   whitecaps and terns diving

"The Universal Fabric of the World,"
   an act of faith and cartography,
Africa and the Americas in 1570
   unseen but drawn out in detail,
his demons, unseen, as well, named,
   described and equally certain

the dead shark and its busy crabs
   with Demagora are Race Point's
enduring present; not beads
   on a string but spaces opening
their own complexities, Helike's
   and Leon's fond attentiveness

Michael Anania

    I have added this vessel
        to a specific past in which it
    had no part, its place secured
        by an accident of naming,
    by death's certainty
        and the familiarity of grief

    Giovanni reckoning
        resource, labor and reward
    against the remote impositions
        of nations and their powers,
    field work counted out across
        oceans and continents

Walking Home, Summer 1960

As usual, past two in the morning,
the sidewalk beside the fruit stand
wet and broom clean, a hose end
bent over the curb, dripping, a few

bits of leaf and stem in the gutter,
accidental messages, easily read;
love makes us all seem uniquely
capable of deciphering the world;

the walk—Dodge Street to 40th
40th south past Chicken-in-the-Rough,
its enraged rooster's golf club flailing,
the blue Admiral Theatre, Farnam east

past the Red Lion and the Golden Spur,
across to Leavenworth, then east again
down to the Bungalow Inn, south next
on 33rd Street, Mason Street and home.

Michael Anania

In Light of

> *bagnate di eros*
> —Rosita Copioli

gulls' wings describe
the air; sea froth,

the sea; fingers spread,
the reach of person and place;

flight, breath's sudden
moments, wishes inhaled,

songs recalled; how
does it persist, this space,

its familiar warmth,
salt tinged; the self,

an array of particles
briefly suspended here

New Year's Day 2013

for David Harwell

I.

above Empoli, past Vitolini,
sheltered by tall trees, a Romanesque church,
untended, abandoned, a motorcycle
repair shop its remaining piazza;
The Romanesque Churches of Tuscany
doesn't list it, so it is unnamed, unmapped;
piety's labor, stones cut and carted
up from the Arno, now darkened with age,
Santa Maria Something or Other,
martyred, no doubt, the dread description lost,
steadfast, the kindling piled at her feet,
tears and prayers reserved for her torturers,
in the back wall a slotted window catches
the broken light for hay bales and chickens

Michael Anania

II.

we could leave it at that, I suppose, one
more irony, sentimental even,
a vestige we visited by accident,
but there is little ease to it; perhaps
because there is no town, imagining
the scaffolding, plumb lines and numbered blocks,
the clamor of construction is clearer;
hands hardened, bent to chisel, auger and line
the Motoguzzi's exhaust in the chill air
sputtering; what sin was this a penance for?
and payment, the master builder come on foot
from Florence or Siena, pounding in stakes
drawing his strings level, counting the cost,
parts and labor, their measured sanctity

Song

sometimes a leaf
   will tremble
      on its stem, while

everything around
   it lifts and falls
      and lifts again

Michael Anania

To and Fro

for Maxine Chernoff

It was a siphon, of sorts, moving liquid from one place to another—actually, however complexly it turned here and there, moving eventually downward—water, as they say, always seeking its own level. Still, it had a kind of consolation about it, something at once certain and mobile, or certain in its mobility. There would be an ending, of course, when the higher container was emptied, though he supposed he might lift the lower container to the higher position and start the flow all over again, a creative act, Jacob's Ladder, if somewhat ambiguously so.
The proximate world, he thought to himself, full of provisional balancing acts, horizons that reoccur daily, the thin, active but permanent line between sea and sky, white clouds tufted above each of the Cyclades, their promise of landfalls to the weary sailor, *O bright Apollo*. Ardor is itself a kind of order, the day, each day, stirred with it, light seeking, with us, its own level. Well, not quite, he said, recalling the textbook diagram of indirect light, the collisions and refractions against ceilings, walls, mere motes in the air, water droplets, pollen. Brightness is a kind of chaos, then, each interruption leaving something suspended there. Here, at least, nameless events hold sway. For clarity's sake, she wanted to hold a single ray of that "peculiar" light, affection, love even, implicit there.
Is there an easy chair with a hassock in your room in the house of language, a reprieve from all these endless, successive approximations, yet still humming with the pleasures of words, sentences, exclamations? Harbor, shadow,

persimmon, bright leaves, orangery—each relaxing in its own way. Shadows have reclaimed the street, umber, burnt sienna, a few specks of flake white at the corner, possible worlds, Saul, and your field of play, Maxine, the narrow space between fact and artifact, each a necessary proposition. Arthur Dove and Alex Katz come to mind, Callahan, as well. What does the photograph propose that the painting doesn't, both steeped in narrative? Is color argumentative? Music? Well, that's another matter altogether.

Michael Anania

A Shard

light tricks us
 sometimes like
  the I-am-I

begin with
 myself
  and am gone

Late Intinerary

solo il nulla s'accresce
—Leopardi

vague or vagrant,
the lists of night,
stars, constellations,
street lights throbbing,
wishes in their own
soft languages, quick
among the city's
deep murmurings

Michael Anania

Plains Song

for Peter Michelson

hard to imagine, although it's true,
Walt Whitman in the Dakotas
listening to Italian music,

the sun setting yellow over
bluestem and buffalo grass;
Norma's plea, *Casta Diva*,

perfect goddess, give us peace,
a harmony of land and sky,
eleven years before Wounded Knee

As It Were

for Robert Hogg

not quite, he said,
looking back at
his footprints
in the fresh snow

this is what
passes for direction,
I suppose, marks
carelessly left behind

Michael Anania

At Argos

for Stratis Havarias

rock-strewn hillside,
cypress trees, their
trunks stripped of bark,
bitter food, bitter days

the barbarians did
come, waves of them;
from one abyss to another
a small interval of light

Niobe's grief, thousands
of children, not dead but
taken, tears from stone,
songs from bare branches

Cañada Vista

for Rudolfo Anaya

your uncle in the high desert
for weeks at a time, returns
the bed of his pickup truck
full of stones, each one
studied for hours, days even,
with you and your house
in mind, lines the ancients
left there, arranged in sentences
above your hearth, the evening
reddening, our faces turned
to the Sandias, reddening as well,
graced by spirits of family,
desert, mountain and light

Michael Anania

This Broken Song

for Rosemary Catacalos

98 degrees in San Antonio
   today, Rose, the sun breaking,
      now and then, through low clouds;

at the spillway, down river, swifts
   arcing, I imagine, above the foam,
      itself at once sudden and brief;

you are, as you leave us, all
   I remember you to be,
      certain in your affections,

love's insistences, like jazz,
   words that carry us along,
      a solo for tenor sax, certain

and implausible; we are left
   behind, loss all around us;
      who is there now to guide us

into song, to offer us, word
   after word, the place where
      myths collide, our grief

like masa, moving from hand
   to hand, the stone hot to the touch;
      they lean into their work, as we

In Time

lean today toward you, your voice
    inflected by Mexico, Coltrane, Miles,
        Greece even, the plaza, open now,

The Espada, all those devotions
    you presided over; can we talk it
        through, in your name, petal

after petal, straining with
    the day's heat, this morning's
        dew still held there, the slap

of tortillas, like castanets, dance,
    hands clapping; laughter, you said,
        is a kind of song, weeping, as well;

reach back to us, just once, the day's
    threads spun through your fingers,
        our singing, brightly colored there

Michael Anania

Riverrun

for Mark Spitzer

1.

you lean into the river
and all its motions,
the long swell, pebbles
smoothed against pebbles,
the grasp at tree roots and marl,
the white undersides of fish
mimicking sunlight on wavelets,
leaf-shaped leeches adrift,
leaves, as well, twigs, and
the soils it carries with it

2.

in Ravenna, in the Baptistry
of San Vitale, the slotted
windows, in place of glass,
have thin panes of marble,
the light they ease inside
thickens, umber, ecru
and yellow going to gold,
exactly what you see
swimming in a river on
a bright day, sun streaked
currents and eddies;
across a small garden
the sages stand in
their golden fire still

3.

older than time or sacrament
a spotted alligator gar eases
through river grasses, its long
snout lifted, occasionally, above
the river's dark surface, neither
saint nor sage, a creature,
like us, of water, silt and light;
any moment is worth its
blessing, all that is known
but unseen, the endless
tumult that shapes us

"Oppi, ne metuas ..."

Carved into the tomb's
brow, a cautionary note.
"Having created a town,
it would be foolish
to waste your time in fear
of Lethe or Lethans' glare;
keep in mind, instead,
the endless joys of living."

In which of her guises do you
meet her, Lygdamus, fresh
sun-warmed soil or the dark hour—
"goddess refrain from naming me"—
dreaded waves beneath the Etruscan
stream, contemplating strife in
an insane world; O that I might be
afraid of nothing in this imaginary
fever, trail a relaxed hand through pale
Tuscan waters, so much child's play,
easing my pulse and my breath,
uiuite felices, memoras et uiuite nostri,
be happy in your life, live and remember.

IV

Hours and Days

I.

you pull the tassel down to you,
your hands yellow with pollen,
yank it out and the broad, trembling
leaves spatter your face with dew

Michael Anania

II.

cucumbers, like green welts
along the long furrows you
stoop over, waddling from one
to another, their fine transparent
thorns caught in your palms

III.

halfway inside the three-ring
cast-iron American furnace,
you tap at the seal between
the rings until it cracks and starts
to break free, fine coal dust everywhere
and the blood smell of exposed rust

IV.

squeeze the peeled shrimp between
your iodine swollen finger
and thumb and the tissue above
the vein strains toward your knife's edge
and splits open from head to tail

V.

over weld lines on the spinning drum
rebars dance like reeds in the wind;
the treadle engages with a thunk
and the great blade descends;
everything jumps; you reach in,
pull the cut rods out, a half-step,
lift, circle back, push down, let go
and the middle of the steel sheaf
is drawn out and falls, forty feet
of it, into a bright-edged, even bundle

VI.

depending on its diameter
bending steel sighs, groans or hums,
and its flake lifts and gathers
into drifts like grey, sooted snow

"The people know the present."

(Cavafy, here, quoting Philostratus.)
Or do we? Yellow trumpet flowers
nod against my stone wall, live

oak shadows sway there, as well;
a jogger's pony tail bobs by, voices,
words, perhaps, but at this distance,

mere noise; there is a breeze today,
tires hum in passing, the purple weight
of beauty berries tugs at their stems,

broad, pale leaves fidget into the light.
These things propose me, propose
my present, moment by moment,

but is that the present Philostratus
had in mind for me, momentary
and contingent? Probably not.

His present was a larger condition,
conditions even, in which my
present is an unlikely participant;

"people know" proposes a collection
of presents, other trees' shadows,
other walls; that present is at best

Michael Anania

an area of time, a bundling
of moments we presume that we share.
The breeze has freshened and the trees

are moving in concert now; the most
active of the beauty berries bobs along
like the bouncing ball above

the lyrics in a movie sing-along,
offering, at least, a nostalgia
for something like unison; melody

is, after all, a kind of shared purpose.
"I envy you," she said, "your chance
of death," an end to all these presents,

the song's expected period, each of us
breathing freely once again, the darkness
and all that the bright screen shared.

It is what holds us, time's chrysalis,
what we emerge from, stretching
into the light and its discreet moments.

Reprieve

> *a little drunk on air*
> —Charles Tomlinson

the limbs of my own
oak trees are stirring
this November morning,

and their shadows churn
the grass's fading autumn
green with wavering light:

simplicity tilts toward me,
all the public bile forestalled
for just a moment or so

Michael Anania

First Snow

after David Travis

you taste it first,
a slight sting in the air,
then the sudden plural
surrounding your breath, bare
branches blossoming white;

put your tongue out, catch
one hexagon there—each shape
unique—and feel it vanish,
late autumn's Pentecost
unspoken, silent

Heading Out

for Cynthia Gallaher

winter trees, the sidewalk's damp
overnight, gone crystalline, wind,
faces wrapped tight and turned

downward; the day scuffs along;
Chicago, its weights counted out
in negative numbers, minus,

below, the less than nothing,
you press yourself against, still
the blue sky, steam-flaked, shines

Michael Anania

At Purchase

for Ed and Elaine

She stretches her legs
into the late October
afternoon sun, her tan slacks

hiked up a bit; Dubuffet
through the low trees,
Pomadoro's columns

unfashioning themselves,
Ernst's makeshift royalty
opens out its own dense

shadows, Rickey's vanes
poised in the still air;
on another bench Segal's

strangers in postures of defensive
loneliness propose a city square,
pigeons and desperate traffic

onto the green, well-tended
lawn where Giacometti's
purposeful citizens stride as though

needing to be somewhere else.
I like to come out here, she says,
especially when it's warm like this

In Time

and feel the sun on my face,
and, she says,—pointing
at the white socks pushed

into the tops of her shoes
—my ankles. It's restful.here,
so much of a certain quiet.

Michael Anania

Idle Thoughts in Troubled Circumstances

I.

if I tilt my head, just so,
the doorframe is parallel
to the grout line on the floor

which itself proposes a unique
form of navigation, vertical
and horizontal fixed, myself

at sea here and solely variable;
I could, of course, make too much
of this, so much else moving

around me, January light
mottled on the window shade,
Schubert at this moment insistent

II.

is it a condition
or a consequence,
this moment of light,

moving water, like music
"momentary in the mind,"
its furtive architectures

at once predictable
and strange, the spaces
it fills, passing certainties,

this impromptu's arc, its
arches, naves and choirs
dissolving hand to hand

Michael Anania

III.

the great asset of poetry
is persistent change,
the torque of one moment

giving way to another,
hand, eyelid, or cloth lifted,
cloud-forms as likely as

any other landscape, purity
ground from lapis, sea
and sky, syllables, notes

fingered into place, our
places, in the song at least,
fixed, moveable and uncertain

In Myriads

for Lucas Klein

ten thousand mountains,
imagine, range after range;
the dead confuse us with
their persistence, more so
it seems than mere memory
might readily explain away;

ten thousand grasses already
cool with dew, swallows
and sparrows are silent;
ghost mirrors and the edges
of divinity go back to their
own pasts where they belong;

ten thousand miles of thick
shadows: to plant by hand is
to grieve over past concerns,
the chill of damp soil, taint
of all the loss it must contain;
think of sunlight and flowering;

ten thousand days, wandering;
the nights turn; their wishes
sustain us, rivers, streams,
clouds reshaping themselves;
nothing is warmed in the moon's
sad steps; where shall I turn to now?

Michael Anania

ten thousand sorrows, songs;
grief proposes an antique string
instrument to give shape to their
emptiness, its face cracked, its
hand-painted rose, still red
untuned and blossoming;

ten thousand fancies or more;
consider the breeze turning
the curtains, the moving limbs
they flex and unflex, arms
and thighs within the night's
warm breath enraptured there

ten thousand, a number merely,
arbitrary and essential, willow
trees or maples, each one has
its part, like thread or string,
the strand of bright water adding
its volume to the silvery stream

A Redbud in Central Ohio

for Judith Moffett

sudden pink, a rush
   that leaves it somewhat
      out of focus, morning's
counterpart, more roseate
   than the midwestern sky
      ever quite manages;
this Eos greets the still
   wintery world's fallow
      fields and bare branches

Michael Anania

Another Iowa Homage

after Angelo Ray

He remained certain of
unconditional love,
and confession, syllables,

in theory, naked. Silva
runs down the hall
[I thought at first,

it was "saliva runs
down the hall," a more
interesting, if some-

what surreal, figure],
the bus window stretching
like clouds and gestures,

the courtyards of Ottoman
houses, playful until
the last engine takes refuge

amid acorns and oak saplings.
Something grows immense,
her fingernails suspended

in thin air. It must have
been a Saturday. Someone
put out an arm, dusty

with sleep. On Sicilian
shores, an undergraduate
writes and stars in innovative,

insightful theatre. She is
where she is, mourning
her first love, poetry.

Michael Anania

Omaha Appendices VII

Family stories can, without any specific
telling or beginning, simply exist,
like the smells of tooth powder and hand soap,
garlic, oregano and basil,
lilac talcum powder and Lucky Tiger,
Bull Durham and Lucky Strikes,
how a kitchen match would sputter,
then flare from my father's thumbnail,
so the story about my grandfather
shooting and killing some guy, midday,
at 16th and Farnam Streets, there
in the heart of downtown Omaha
was an unquestioned part of my life,
something I knew without recalling it.
He was not, the story said, arrested
or charged but had to go to Portland—
Maine, not Oregon, as I once thought—
where he worked as a welder in a shipyard.
When he came back, he slept for a time
on the daybed in our living room
and had, I remember, whiskey
or dago red with a raw egg in it
for breakfast, the yolk turned orange
by the wine, like a harvest moon
descending, and he would smile at my stare
and wipe his mouth with his thick hand.
The story, as it turns out, was not true
or rather not entirely true. The First
National Bank building had offices
above the bank with an entrance

on Farnam Street. A cousin of ours,
a Sacco, and a lawyer were moving
from a car toward the offices' entrance
when my grandfather stepped up,
gun drawn and pulled the trigger
three or four times, click click click.
No shots were fired. The police assumed
that the gun had misfired and planned
to charge him with attempted murder
or at least assault with a deadly weapon,
but the gun had no magazine, so was
not a deadly weapon and my grandfather
who had not fled was never charged.
Sacco decided to forego the deposition
the lawyer had scheduled . "Show's over,
move along," the cop probably said
to the gathering crowd. Whether he was
taken into custody or merely went home
with his empty gun the newspaper
account I found a few years ago
doesn't say. Why Portland, Maine?
no version of the story ever explained
or why leave at all since he wasn't charged.
Out of sight, out of mind, my mother
would say in lieu of saying nothing
though I can't help thinking of Northrup Jones,
the bakery next door to the bank entrance
with gold foil block lettering above
a window full of cakes on cake stands,
gleaming pies, donuts and strudels.

Michael Anania

Omaha Appendices VIII

This is my earliest memory—
in a playpen in "the little house,"
the one-room house on Rees Street,
where we lived until I was three,
my mother at the kitchen sink,
her usual whistling, the colored beads
between the wooden slats turning,
the trapdoor down to the basement
summer kitchen was propped open,
screams and the basement screen
door slammed, noise on the ladder,
my Aunt Jenny bobbing into the room
slams the trapdoor shut and pulls
our one chair onto it, sits shouting
help to my mother, my grandfather
below her, cursing in Calabrese,
bangs the underside of the trapdoor,
my mother with her in the chair,
the chair now bouncing, Jenny tall
and thin with long, wavy chestnut hair,
my mother short and blonde, Jenny's
brown eyes made larger by her thick
glasses, my mother's bright blue eyes,
wide, her curled hair sprung up and down
as the chair bounced again and again
above his fury, the whole house
shaking, the playpen, the chair, faces,
everything all at once shattering.

V
A Prologue and Songs from a Libretto

In 2017 Jeff Plankenhorn—singer, guitarist, and composer—asked me if I would consider writing the lyrics for a staged concert drama which he would score. Thinking of Jeff's well-known song "Trouble" ("Don't want no trouble but trouble finds me") and the outlaw legends surrounding blues musicians, I proposed a blues opera, based on Gay's The Beggars Opera *and Brecht and Weil's* Three Penny Opera, *in which Mac Heath is a blues musician, and Polly is the daughter of a music publisher. A few of the lyrics were scored, but Jeff's career went elsewhere, and the project was set aside. These lyrics are part of what remains of the Blues Opera.*

Prologue

Listen up! Brothers and sisters, listen up.
Tonight you're gonna hear an opera (imagine that!)
Full of pickers and wailers and crooked jailers,
Downright thieves and stand alone grifters.
It's about the blues, easy sorrow and hard won joy,
Something lifted in song out of love and loss,
Robert Johnson, remember him, and Blind Lemon,
Muddy Waters, Little Walter and Bobby Blue Bland,
Foot-worn galleries, outdoor kitchens, chickens in the yard,
And our bluesman, a Creole Cajun with bayou in his veins,
Mac the Heathen, outlaw picker, shuffleman, thief.
String bending, wife stealing, no doubt about it,
And a murderer, they say. All across the territories
They find a widow, flat broke, heartsick and smiling
Or a man pig-stuck in the mud at the side of the road.
It's Mac Heath they blame but never pursue.
A hero? Well, I guess that depends entirely
On whether you're pig stuck or smiling.

Michael Anania

Sad Eyes and Smiles

You leave because you have no choice,
   Dust on the road, dust in your voice.
With sad eyes and a sadder smile.
   She says, Stay just a little while?

You can bend a string, touch a heart,
   Always sweet and pure at the start,
Count through the song, count out the miles,
   Dust in your throat, sad eyes and smiles.

Chicory coffee, cornbread in a bowl
   A calloused hand to soothe your soul,
Damp hair tangled, a bluebird barrette,
   A faded house dress, hard to forget.

You can bend a string, break a heart,
   Bittersweet, wrong from the start,
Sing to the dashboard, count out the miles,
   Caught where you live, sad eyes and smiles.

Morning haze, fresh oil on the road,
   Sometimes the blues is a heavy load,
Linoleum flowers, lavender soap,
   Making love is its own kind of hope.

You move with ease from fret to fret,
   From song to song, from joy to regret;
Town after town, kiss sweetened miles,
   Caught in your heart, sad eyes and smiles.

Polly's first song

I could forget my father's greed
And my mother's endless screaming.
I could forget my pettiness
And nights of sinful dreaming.
   All that I ever wanted
   Glowed like a spark inside me.

How do we know what makes us whole,
What parts are the parts we need,
What sins are our essential sins
In thought or word or deed.
   All that I ever dreamed of
   Stirred like a flame inside me.

I had imagined love would be
Something pure and clean and bright.
Now it seems to be made of earth
And the dampness of the night.
   All that I ever reached for,
   Burns like flame inside me.

It's smell and taste and grasping;
It's a breath that's not your own.
You hear it lift beside you
And hear it when you're alone.
   All that I thought I'd die for
   Roars like a fire inside me.

Michael Anania

I used to wish upon a star,
Count the petals on a flower.
Now I wait for him each night,
Counting minutes into hours.
 All that my wishes wished for
 Sears its flame at every pore.

Mac's Confession

Whenever they asked me
About all those murders,
Guns and knives and sash cords,
I'd just take a long pull
On my bottle, smile and tilt
My head into a song,
Killin's good for the blues,
Like a bent-over hat
And a scratched-up guitar,
A thick hand and a razor scar.
Nothing washes off easier
Than someone else's dirt
Or feels any better than
Someone else's hurt.

They say I've killed people
In places I've never been,
Pig-stuck husbands, jailers
Left slumped in their cells,
Bankers and ribbon clerks,
Any fool who crossed me.
Killin's good for the blues,
Like a bent-over hat
And a scratched-up guitar,
A thick hand and a razor scar.
Nothing washes off easier
Than someone else's dirt
Or feels any better than
Someone else's hurt.

Michael Anania

Being genuine or gen-u-ine's
A kind of work that wears
On you like a rough road,
You stiffen up and ache
From the long shake of it
It thickens in your throat.
Killin's good for the blues,
Like a bent-over hat
And a scratched-up guitar,
A thick hand and a razor scar.
Nothing washes off easier
Than someone else's dirt
Or feels any better than
Someone else's hurt.

Polly's Song

Wishes and dreams. Dreams and wishes.
I'd like to reach across the sky,
And touch more than I ever imagined.

I think love is a hand among the stars,
Bright, perfected by the dark,
Sparks of touch, meteor showers.

Myself bright and awakening,
Adrift with me there, fireflies
Above this summer's flowers.

Wishes and dreams. Dreams and wishes,
Blown among constellations,
A zodiac busy between us.

Michael Anania

Duet (Mac and Polly)

Polly

With you, watching the turning stars,
We are sheltered by the night.
Touched by string-worn fingers;
I am the song, my love's delight.
    It's like the coffee lady said.
    "It's better when it's good."

Mac

The night is filled, every single night,
With what the bending string recalls,
Remembered sighs and sorrows,
All that's been lost, all that falls.
    It's like the old card dealer said,
    "It's better when it's good."

Polly

Look there, Cassiopeia calls,
A torch singer singing in the dark
Of love and love's persistence,
Of passion and passion's spark.
    It's like the spinning lady said,
   "It's better when it's good."

Mac

I see a pulsing light, the mark
In time of a distant flame.
How can it matter to us?
Is it any more than a name?
   It's like the old junk dealer said,
  "It's better when it's good."

Polly

Hold me a moment. We're the same,
Fiercely bright stars in a starry sky.
Doubt is just the empty space we
Cross each night with ease and sigh.
   It's like the constant lover said,
  "It's better when it's good."

Both

It's better when the world's forgot.
Touch is the night's reprieve.
Starlight is a garden, then,
Where fire and flower weave
And bind themselves together
As no one thought they could.
The blues is a kind of joy tonight.
It's better when it's good.

Michael Anania

Jenny's Song

There is nothing in this city but pain,
Where the pimps and the dealers are in charge.
It's your stuff that they want, but they'll take your soul
And they'll laugh as they throw it in the dirt.
Cause it's not the souls or money they need
What they feed on is someone else's hurt

But a coupe with a nailhead
And twin glasspacks comes roaring
Just to carry me away.

When I was a girl I lived at the end
Of a dirt track where everything was grey.
We heard about a war, and my father went,
I remember him walking toward the town,
And my mother slamming the screen door shut
And the wind turning the sky from blue to brown.

Then a coupe with a nailhead
And twin glasspacks came roaring,
Just to take me away.

When I think of the past and my childish self
I get dizzy over everything I've lost,
Not the Baptists or blackstrap molasses,
Or the bitterness that hovered like a cloud
But how I could find my way through a song
Like something I could dream for out loud.

And a coupe with a nailhead
And twin glasspacks came roaring
Just to take me away.

Now I wait at the door, the blues at my back
With a welt of red neon on my cheek.
Crack skinny, I'm just a part in the show
For the swells and their girls walking by,
It's what they all come for, the wages of sin,
And a sorrow they can rent, steal or try.

Til the coupe with a nailhead,
And twin glasspacks comes roaring,
And carries me away.

Michael Anania

Dancer's Song

I got a boogie woogie wallet
  Won it up at the fair,
Got a boogie woogie wallet
  Won it up at the fair,
Want a boogie woogie woman,
  Take her everywhere.

Well, beat me daddy,
  Beat me eight to the bar,
Yeah, beat me daddy,
  Beat me eight to the bar,
With a boogie woogie woman and a
  Sears Roebuck guitar.

My wallet's got dancers,
  Pink yellow and blue,
Yeah, my wallet's got dancers
  Pink, yellow and blue,
They're electric dancers
  Just like me and you.

Come dance with me baby
  Under this neon sign,
Come dance with me baby
  Under this neon sign,
We'll drink 7-Up with
  Mogen David wine.

Think I'll grow me a moustache
  Go to New Orleans,
Think I'll grow me a moustache,
  Go to New Orleans,
With my boogie woogie wallet
  Bulging in my jeans.

I got a boogie woogie wallet,
  Take it everywhere;
I got a boogie woogie wallet,
  Take it everywhere.
Come on let's boogie,
  Got no time to spare.

Notes

"Instead of"—"*e stato un piacere ... Maurizio*": It was a pleasure to hear your voice, Maurizio. Maurizio Marchini, Italian tenor, who sang "Nessun Dorma" from his balcony in Florence during the pandemic lockdown.

"All This While"—epigraph from *Allegri*, translated by Geoffrey Brock.

"Your Fancy and Your Sight"—Actaeon: Actaeon, the hunter, saw Diana bathing. She transformed him into a stag, so the hunter was hunted. The sweet owl of Suffolk and smooth Hesperus were common Elizabethan formulae.

"Gli Ucelli"—"kaladóon," "hirundo": swallows. Fermi and Respighi did sail together from Rio to Genoa, and Fermi did ask the question about music and physics. One of Fermi's student papers was on the physics of sound.

"Six Variations on a Theme by Robert Schumann"—"Variations of the Name Abegg."

"Memory Songs"—The Demegora jar is in the Oriental Institute in Chicago. "Giovanni, Johannes": Giovanni Anania (1957–2015), Professor of Economics, specializing in agricultural resources, University of Calabria. Johannes Laurentius Anania (1545–1607), Calabrian cartographer and demonologist,. His works include *De Naturum Daemonum* and a world map.

"In Light of"—"*bagnate di eros*": love's moisture, probably from Sappho (in Italian "and you bathed yourself in eros.")

"At Argos"—"waves of them": the barbarians, first the Germans in WWII, then the Russians in the Civil War, who kidnapped thousands of Greek children. In Cavafy's much earlier, ironic poem, the barbarians never come.

"Cañada Vista"—the site of Rudolfo Anaya's house above Albuquerque.

"*Oppi, ne metuas* ..." (do not be afraid)—two funerary inscriptions, the first Roman, the second Etruscan.

"At Purchase"—the Donald M. Kendall Sculpture Gardens at Purchase, NY.

"In Myriads"—Much of its imagery is borrowed from Lucas Klein's translations of Yi Shangyin.

"Another Iowa Homage"—Found in an issue of the *Iowa Review*.

"Jenny's Song"—Verse and refrain are wholly based on "Pirate Jenny," Jenny Diver's song by Kurt Weil and Bertold Brecht in *The Threepenny Opera*.

Acknowledgments

Grateful acknowledgement is made to the following publications in which some of these poems first appeared: *Taint Taint Taint, Café Review, Notre Dame Review, Fortnightly Review, Voices de la Luna, Colorado Review, Canvas Hat, New American Writing, Iowa Review, Denver Quarterly, Toad Suck Review, Nude Bruce Review,* and *Best American Poetry.*

About the Author

MICHAEL ANANIA was born in Omaha, Nebraska, and studied at the University of Nebraska and the University at Buffalo. He is a poet, essayist, and fiction writer. His published work includes fifteen collections of poetry, among them *Selected Poems* (1994), *Heat Lines* (2006), *Continuous Showings* (2017), and *Nightsongs and Clamors* (2018). His work is widely anthologized and has been translated into Italian, German, French, Spanish, and Czech. He has also published a novel, *The Red Menace*, and a collection of essays, *In Plain Sight*. A critical volume, *From the Word to the Place: Essays on the Work of Michael Anania*, edited by Lea Graham, was published by Mad Hat in 2022.

Anania was poetry editor of *Audit, a quarterly*, founder and co-editor of *Audit/Poetry*, poetry and literary editor of The Swallow Press, poetry editor of *Partisan Review*, and a contributing editor to *Tri-Quarterly* and has served as as an advisory editor to a number of other magazines and presses, including Dalkey Archive, Wesleyan University Press, and FCII.

He is Professor Emeritus of English at the University of Illinois at Chicago and a member of the faculty in writing at Northwestern University. He has also taught at the University at Buffalo and the University of Chicago. He lives in Austin, Texas, and on Lake Michigan.

www.ingramcontent.com/pod-product-compliance
Lightning Source LLC
Chambersburg PA
CBHW020334170426
43200CB00006B/383